Preserve Your Family History

A Step-by-Step Guide for Interviewing Family Members and Writing Oral Histories

LeAnn R. Ralph

ISBN-13 978-1-60145-239-9
ISBN-10 1-60145-239-X

Published by LeAnn R. Ralph; E6689 970th Ave; Colfax, WI 54730 USA.

Printed in the United States of America.

Booklocker.com, Inc.
2007

Preserve Your Family History

A Step-by-Step Guide for Interviewing Family Members and Writing Oral Histories

LeAnn R. Ralph

Table of Contents

Introduction

If you think you need "extra-special literary talent" to write your family stories, think again.

All you really need is a willingness to listen, a list of people to interview, a set of questions to ask, a tape recorder, a pen, a notepad, and a computer (or even a typewriter will do).

By the time you have finished following the instructions in *Preserve Your Family History (A Step-by-Step Guide for Interviewing Family Members and Writing Oral Histories)*, you will have a collection of stories from your grandmother and grandfather, mother and father, or aunts and uncles that you can share with other family members—and that you can leave for future generations. Just imagine how much your great-great-great-great grandchildren are going to enjoy reading about the lives of their ancestors.

In the process of gathering those stories, you will also learn more about your own history: where you come from, what has shaped your values, opinions and attitudes and how you fit into your family structure.

At the very least, you will have wonderful conversations with family members. You will also give those people an opportunity to share some of their past and the wisdom that they have accumulated over a lifetime.

And eventually, when your loved ones pass on, you will have the satisfaction of knowing that their stories are not lost forever.

LeAnn R. Ralph
Colfax, Wisconsin

Part I

Everyone Has a Story to Tell

"Everyone has a story to tell."

It might sound like a cliché—but it's true. After working as a newspaper reporter for nearly 10 years, I know that everyone does, indeed, have a story to tell.

Consider the gentleman and his wife, who, when they retired from dairy farming in Wisconsin, built a house on a portion of their acreage and then developed cross-country ski trails that run along a creek. The trails are open to anyone and everyone. Free of charge. Complete with pairs of cross-country skis that people can borrow if they don't have their own. Each year, the husband and wife pay for an advertisement in local newspapers inviting their neighbors and other community members to go cross-country skiing on their property. Why? As it turns out, many years ago, the man was a championship ski-jumper, and he and his wife want to introduce others to the joys of skiing.

And then there's the group of people who meet at a municipal hall in a tiny village in Wisconsin once a week to enjoy ballroom dancing. Some of them drive as far as 75 miles one way—rain, snow, wind, below zero temperatures—nothing stops them. These folks are in their 60s, 70s, and 80s, and they have energy to spare. They have been enjoying their dances at the municipal hall for years, and each one of them has a story to tell about how they learned to dance and where their dancing has taken them.

There's also the artist who lives in the country and paints wildlife watercolors. On a winter day, 200 wild turkeys visit her backyard in rural Wisconsin to enjoy the corn she has put out for them. Deer, pheasants and song birds also call her property home, as do a number of cats she had rescued from various situations. She, too, has a story to tell about why she left her job at a university to become a full-time artist and of the struggles and financial hardships she endured until her paintings began to sell.

But even before I started working as a journalist, I knew that life experiences make interesting stories. And I didn't have to look any farther than my own family.

My father was born in 1914, and my mother was born in 1916. They lived during a time of enormous change. They went from farming with horses to farming with tractors. They started out milking cows by hand and ended up milking cows with milking machines run by electricity. My mother gave birth to my brother and sister at home. I was born in a hospital. They also experienced many historical events: the Great Depression and World War II and Americans landing on the moon.

As I was growing up, my mother and father would tell stories about their childhoods. Mom was the daughter of Norwegian immigrants, and her grandfather homesteaded our dairy farm in Wisconsin in the late 1800s. Dad was the son of German and Scottish immigrants. When my father was a little boy, his parents worked as cooks in a lumber camp in northern Wisconsin.

Much to my regret, I never asked Mom and Dad to sit down with a tape recorder and tell their stories. My mother died in 1985 at the age of 68. My father passed away in 1992 at the age of 78. The majority of their stories, except for the few that I remember, are lost forever.

If you are willing to apply the techniques I learned during my years as a newspaper reporter about interviewing people and writing their stories, your family stories do not have to share the same fate.

And of course, you can also use the interview techniques and the questions to interview friends and neighbors to capture their stories as well.

****

Part II

Step-by-Step Instructions & Tips
For Gathering & Writing Your Family Stories

1. Decide which people you would like to interview.

Sit down with a sheet of paper and make a list. The list could include Grandma and Grandpa, Mom and Dad, Aunt and Uncle. Or, if you want to include more people, consider interviewing neighbors or other community members who could contribute to the history of the area, or people who have been good friends of your family members.

Depending upon the number of stories you want to write and the amount of time you want to devote to the project, your list can be as short as only one person or as long as every adult member in your family, as well as friends and neighbors and other community members. Your manuscript of completed stories could be 10 pages long—or 500 pages.

You also do not necessarily have to write the stories. Even if you only record the interviews, you still will have a record of those stories.

2. Ask for permission to conduct an interview.

Select which person you want to interview first, and then tell that person about your plan to write— or tape record—a collection of family stories (or community stories) and ask for permission to do the interview.

If the answer is 'no' perhaps that person thinks he or she has nothing worthwhile to say. You have two choices at this point: either go ahead and ask another person, or give the first person time to think about the idea. Chances are that after the person who initially said 'no' has had time to think and consider, he or she may agree to talk to you.

Several times while I was working as a newspaper reporter, people said they did not want to be interviewed, but after thinking about it for a while, changed their minds. And the interviews turned out to be just as good, if not better, than interviews conducted with people who had agreed right away.

On the other hand, if the person absolutely, positively refuses to be interviewed, perhaps you can find another family member or a friend who can tell you something about that person. If so, you might be able to use it to your advantage. You could go back to Uncle George (just as an example), and say, "Mary Smith told me that the two of you used to walk to school together and that one time, when Mary fell down in the mud, you rescued her." This might be enough to change Uncle George's mind about being interviewed. Or it might not.

In the end, if someone really does not want to be interviewed, respect his or her decision and move on to another person. It's still possible he or she will agree to the interview later on.

3. Set a formal date and time for the interview.

Setting a date and time for the interview will give your interviewee an opportunity to mentally prepare and to remember stories.

While I was working as a newspaper reporter, people appreciated having several days or a week to consider what they would want to say during the interview.

Think back to a time when someone asked you a question right out of the blue but you weren't quite sure how to answer it. You fumbled your way through, and then later on, the perfect answer popped into your head and you thought to yourself, "Why did I say *that*? I should have said *this*."

When people know they have time to prepare and to think and to reflect, they feel more confident about being interviewed.

4. Provide a list of questions several days or weeks before the interview.

Providing a list of questions also will give your interviewee time to remember stories. And it will help you to organize your interview. The interview will go more smoothly if you know which questions you want to ask rather than leaving it all to chance.

In my experience as a newspaper reporter, just about every time I called someone to set up an interview, he or she would say, "what are you going to ask me about?" Even if I only gave them a general idea of the questions, they felt more relaxed about doing the interview.

Now that I'm an author, I can also speak to this issue from first-hand experience. When my first book, *Christmas in Dairyland (True Stories from a Wisconsin Farm)* (visit http://ruralroute2.com for more information) was published in August of 2003, I was completely unprepared when the first newspaper reporter called me for an interview. "Do you have time to talk now? Good!" she said, and then she began firing questions at me.

When the interview was over, I felt as if I had run a marathon, and of course, later on I thought, "Oh, shoot. I should have said *this* instead of *that*."

Other reporters were more thoughtful and called in advance to set up a time to conduct the interview and also told me what questions they were planning to ask. The interviews went more smoothly, and I know that I gave better answers.

Help your interviewee to give you good stories for your family history by providing a list of questions before the interview. You will both benefit.

5. Focus on a single subject or event in each list of questions.

School, holidays (Christmas, Thanksgiving, Fourth of July), birthdays, seasons (spring, summer, winter, fall), best friends, hobbies, siblings, marriage, occupation, childhood home, adult home, hometown, illnesses…the possibilities are nearly endless.

While working as a newspaper reporter, I found that it was best to ask all of my questions about one subject while we were on that subject. Going back later to clarify a point or two is fine, but if the questions are too scattered, the information from the interview will end up scattered as well, and it will be more difficult to write a cohesive story.

Focusing on a single subject or event in each list of questions will also help your interviewee to organize his or her thoughts and to remember more details and stories.

Lists of questions for 30 different subjects are included below which you can use 'as is' or which you can use to help you generate your own questions.

6. Use the 'who, what, where, when, how, and why' strategy when formulating your questions.

"Who was your best friend?" "What was the most fun you had with your best friend?" "When did you get to see your best friend?" "How did you and your best friend meet?" "Why was this person your best friend?"

Using this strategy to ask questions will ensure that you approach the subject from all angles. Asking a question in one form might not yield much of a story, but if the question is asked in a different way, the story that emerges could be just what you were hoping for.

7. Ask open-ended questions and not 'yes or no' or 'one word answer' questions.

"What form of transportation did you use to get to school?" or "What route did you take to get to school?" is better than "Did you walk to school when you were growing up?"

If you ask, "did you walk to school," you are likely to receive a 'yes or no' answer, and once that happens, it's more difficult to get back on track with details. It's almost as if by answering "yes" or "no," the person thinks he or she has already given you a complete answer and is ready to move on to the next question.

Asking 'yes or no' questions and 'one-word-answer' questions also sets you up to ask another 'yes or no' or 'one-word-answer' question. Question: "Did you walk to school when you were a kid?" Answer: "No." Question: "How *did* you get to school?" Answer: "Bus."

Asking "what transportation did you use to get to school?" or "what route did you take to get to school?" gives the interviewee an opportunity to talk about modes of transportation or the routes taken to school as well as the ways in which the transportation or the route to school may have changed at different times of the year or during different years.

Here's another way to think about it. If I asked you, "what color was your bedroom when you were growing up," how would you answer? You'd probably say something like "blue," or "pink" or maybe "yellow." (My room was blue, by the way.)

But if I asked you "what are your most vivid memories associated with your room when you were growing up?" then how would you answer? For me, the answer would be my big sister. She is 19 years older than I am, and she worked for the electric cooperative that supplied electricity to our farm and to many other rural areas in our county. We shared a room, and I enjoyed watching her get ready for work. Putting on perfume and lipstick and styling her hair were fascinating processes, as far as I was concerned. I was too squirmy, myself, to enjoy sitting still while my mother put rollers in *my* hair, but I enjoyed watching Loretta fix her own hair.

8. Use a tape recorder to record the interview.

Taping the interview will help you gather details that you might miss if you are only taking notes. Recording direct quotes requires a quick ear and an even faster pen.

Using a tape recorder also will allow you to listen more closely so that you can ask clarifying questions, rather than spending pauses in the conversation to catch up on writing your notes.

Use 60 minute tapes, rather than 90 minute tapes. The 60 minute tapes will hold up better over time and will retain better sound quality.

Make a note on the cassette about who is being interviewed, the date, and whether it is part 1 or part 2 of the interview.

Just as you begin taping, introduce yourself as the interviewer and then introduce the speaker; also identify the date and time of the interview. If you plan to interview several people, this will help you to know who is speaking on any given tape.

Identifying the interviewer, the speaker, the date and the time will also help others know what is on the tape years from now. The note you made on the cassette could wear off or become smeared, so this is a way to make sure the identities of the speakers are not lost.

When you turn the tape over during the interview, identify the speaker and say that it is part 2 of the interview ("Joe Smith interview; part 2").

Also be sure to note on the cassette that it is part 2 of the interview. This will help you to know that there is an interview on the other side so you can avoid taping over an interview.

If you want to take notes during the interview, that's fine too. Notes will help you remember what you talked about and will give you an idea of where a particular subject or question is located on the tape.

Another advantage of tape recording the interview is that you don't have to write the story immediately. Since the whole interview is on tape, you can work on the story when it's convenient for you.

If you rely only on notes but can't work on the manuscript for several days or a week, or maybe longer, you'll find that you can't remember the details as well as you would have if you had worked on it right away.

Or, as I mentioned earlier, if you only want to record the interviews, you will still have a record of the stories. If you have access to videotaping equipment, and the person you are interviewing is agreeable to being videotaped, you also could videotape the interview.

9. Chat about something else for a while if the person you are interviewing seems nervous at the prospect of being tape-recorded.

Many times while working as a newspaper reporter, I found that people would become nervous as soon as I turned on the tape recorder. But, if I made a comment about the weather or asked about their flower gardens or an interesting picture on the wall, they would respond, and within a minute or two, would stop looking at the tape recorder. Then I could start the 'real' interview.

In most instances, after you begin the interview, your interviewee will soon relax and won't even notice the tape recorder.

You could also tape your introduction and play it back for the person you are interviewing. "This is interview number three, part 1, on August 29, 2007, and I am interviewing Edna Green. Edna is my dad's great-aunt. She is my dad's *favorite* great-aunt!"

Rewind the tape and play it for Great-aunt Edna. Then you could say, "I always think I sound so different on tape. Other people tell me that's how I sound to them, but that's not how I sound to myself." Great-aunt Edna might agree that's how you sound to her, and she might want to know how *she* sounds. This might be enough to break the ice and help Great-aunt Edna to relax about being tape recorded.

10. Transcribe the tape and write up your notes.

Sophisticated computer software with voice recognition capabilities can transcribe your interviews for you. From what I've read, however, the computer software doesn't always work well (instead of "six or eight pies," the software may translate it as "six a rate eyes" or instead of "We liked to watch Pa and Ma Kettle, it will translate into, "We liked to watch Palmyra Tuttle).

But this is not a book about purchasing expensive computer equipment and software. It's a book that gives you step-by-step instructions on preserving your family history *using skills, materials and supplies that are easily available to anyone.*

When you transcribe the tape, either keep the transcript in a question-and-answer format, or, if you prefer, omit the questions from the transcript and simply record the answers.

Another option is a combination of the two: include clarifying questions where they occur, but for the rest of the story, omit the questions and let the person tell the story in his or her own words.

You may also want to include a paragraph at the beginning of each person's story that identifies the speaker. Here's an example: "Mary Brown is my mother's cousin. At the time of the interview in 2007, she was 85 years old and lived in the same house where she grew up on Four Corners Road."

Transcribing a tape may sound like a daunting task. There's nothing difficult about transcribing a tape, although it can be time consuming. As I mentioned earlier, when you are transcribing a tape, you do not have to complete it all at once. Do as much as time allows. Set a specific amount of time to work at it each day, say 15 minutes or a half an hour. Transcribing a 60-minute tape, for example, may take two or three hours.

When I transcribe a tape, I listen to a sentence or two and then hit the pause button while I type up what was just said.

Another technique involves listening to 5 or 10 minutes of the interview and then going back and listening to a sentence or two, hitting the pause button, and typing the words. This will help you become familiar with what you will be typing before you start to type.

11. Edit the manuscript when you have finished transcribing the tape.

Review what you have typed to see if paragraphs need to be moved around to make it read better. For example, if you asked questions about school, and the person you are interviewing began talking at length about Christmas programs at school and decorating a Christmas tree at school, and then later on, you asked questions about Christmas, it's possible that the school Christmas stories might fit better with the other Christmas stories. This is a judgment call for you, though, and can only be made once you know what stories you have in the manuscript.

Do not be afraid to edit the manuscript if that will help the story. Spoken language—the way people actually talk—is different than the dialogue or quotes you read in books or magazines or newspapers.

Here's an example: "When we were kids, Ma and Dad would take us on picnics. The place we went most of the time was called. . .let's see. . .where was that. . .it was just on the tip of my tongue, too. . .it was someplace in the country. . .we took the horse and buggy. . .I know that because I remember the horse. . .his name was Jake. . .he was black with a white star on his forehead. . .let's see, the place was called. . .hmmm. . .it was called. . .John's Creek. That's it. It was John's Creek. No. Wait. It was Johnson Creek. I remember now because we had neighbors with the last name of Johnson."

If you want to preserve the flavor of the interview, you could leave that passage as it is. Or, if you want to smooth it out, you could edit it to read: "When we were kids, Ma and Dad would take us on picnics. We went by horse and buggy, and the horse was named Jake. He was black with a white star on his forehead. The place we went most of the time was called Johnson's Creek. I remember that because we had neighbors named Johnson."

To get an idea of what is included in an oral history, read one or two of Studs Terkel's oral history books. Terkel's books include *Division Street* (1967), *Hard Times* (1970), *Working* (1974), *The Good War* (1984), *The Great Divide* (1988), and *RACE* (1992).

(If you would like help in editing your manuscript after you have transcribed your tapes, see pages 64 and 65 for details. I will edit your manuscript at a cost of 1 cent per word.)

12. Spread out your interviews.

Consider doing the interview for one person during a couple of shorter sessions rather than one long session. If you have 20 different sets of questions you want to ask, your interviewee may become too tired in one long session to give good answers. And the object is to record as many stories as possible.

While interviewing older people for newspaper stories, I discovered that after a half an hour or an hour—two hours at the most—the person was getting tired and was ready to wrap up the interview.

Spreading out the interviews may also give your interviewee an opportunity to remember more information related to questions that you asked the first time around.

If, however, your interviewee is inclined to keep talking, keep going and don't worry about the time.

13. Print the stories from your computer and put them into a three-ring binder or publish them in another way.

After you have finished all of your interviews, have transcribed the tapes and have edited the manuscript, make multiple copies and give them to family members as gifts. If you interviewed other people who are community members or who are friends of the family, they will probably want a copy as well.

Some craft shops sell book-binding kits, and if you want to take the manuscript a step farther, you might want to print and bind your own books. You can also use the ring-binder type of kits businesses use for their business reports. Depending on how many you buy, the ring-binder kits might cost somewhere around $3 or $4 each.

Or you may want to consider publishing the stories print-on-demand (POD).

If you are certain that a larger audience exists for the stories, so that the number of copies sold will justify the cost of publishing, there are many POD companies, and for a price that starts out at a couple of hundred dollars, you can publish the stories as a trade paperback. To find POD companies, conduct an Internet search with the keywords, 'print-on-demand.'

To determine whether a wider audience exists beyond your family and friends, consider whether the people you interviewed are prominent in the area where you live, such as a local politician, a doctor, a business owner, or a teacher who worked in the local school district and who touched the lives of many people in the area. Or maybe the stories you gathered are particularly compelling because of the history covered, first-hand experiences in World War II or The Great Depression, for example.

If many people in your hometown express interest in the stories and would be likely to purchase a copy of the book, then publishing POD might be worth considering.

The company that I used to publish my books, *Christmas in Dairyland (True Stories from a Wisconsin Farm)*, *Give Me a Home Where the Dairy Cows Roam*, *Cream of the Crop (More True Stories from a Wisconsin Farm)* and *Where the Green Grass Grows (Spring and Summer Stories from a Wisconsin Farm)* and which I would recommend to others, is Booklocker — www.booklocker.com

If you are certain a wider audience exists for your oral history book, check out Booklocker's author's guidelines to see if your book might fit in with their publishing program.

On the following pages, you will find questions to help you with your interviews. All together, there are 30 sets of questions (more than 400 questions in all) covering 30 different subjects. Print out each set of questions and use them 'as is.' Or pick and choose from among the questions. Or use them to help you formulate your own sets of questions.

Many times, people have told me they would like to interview family members or friends or neighbors or community members to get their stories but that they don't know where to start when it comes to asking questions.

Subjects covered in the sets of questions below include hometown, school, brothers/sisters/cousins, mother, father, childhood home, wedding day, spouse/marriage, adult home, children, birthdays, spring, summer, fall/autumn, winter, Easter, Fourth of July, Thanksgiving, Christmas, other holidays, war, pets, hobbies, food, occupation/ work, illness and injuries, friends, neighbors, church/religion and changes.

And remember: this book is meant to be used. Write notes in it. Photo copy the questions. Leave a copy of it with the people you are interviewing so they can read it and find out what questions you might want to ask. Share it with others who want to capture their family stories. Give copies as gifts.

With each day that goes by, more and more stories are lost as people pass away without leaving the rich legacy of their history for the rest of us. But it doesn't have to be that way. And this book can help. Everyone *does* have a story to tell.

****

Part III

Questions

Subject #1: Hometown

1. What is the name of your hometown? Where is it located?

2. Describe your hometown. Large or small? Houses close to the streets? Wide boulevards? Large trees?

3. What were some of the businesses in town when you were growing up? What was your favorite business? Why?

4. Tell me what else you remember about the businesses in your hometown while you were growing up (store, restaurant, movie theater, barber shop).

5. Who are some of the people that you remember from your hometown? What did they look like? When did you see them? What was memorable about those people?

6. Describe any celebrations or holidays in your hometown. Why were they memorable? (Fourth of July; Memorial Day; Christmas; Thanksgiving; Founder's Day; Centennial Celebration)

7. Tell me about anything unusual, interesting or amusing concerning your hometown.

8. What is your hometown's "claim to fame" — what is it "famous" for (if anything)?

Subject #2: School (elementary; high school; post-secondary)

1. Where did you go to school when you were growing up?

2. How did you get to school? What route did you take?

3. Tell me about any amusing, interesting or unusual incidents that happened on your way to or from school.

4. Tell me about any amusing, interesting or unusual incidents that happened at school.

5. Tell me about any amusing, interesting or unusual incidents that happened concerning some of your classmates.

6. What clothes did you wear to school? What was your favorite outfit? Why was it your favorite?

7. How many students were in your class? How many students were in the whole school? How many grades?

8. What was your <u>favorite</u> subject? Why?

9. What was your <u>least-favorite</u> subject? Why?

10. Who was your <u>favorite</u> teacher? Why?

11. Who was your <u>least-favorite</u> teacher? Why?

12. Tell me about your best friend.

13. Tell me about your <u>happiest</u> moments in school. What was your best accomplishment?

14. Tell me about your <u>worst</u> moments in school. Did you learn anything from your worst moments?

15. Where did you attend high school?

16. Tell me about any unusual, interesting or amusing incidents that happened in high school.

17. Who was your <u>favorite</u> high school teacher? Why?

18. Who was your <u>least-favorite</u> high school teacher? Why

19. What was your <u>favorite</u> high school subject? Why?

20. What was your <u>least-favorite</u> high school subject? Why?

21. Tell me about your academic achievements. What was your best academic achievement? What did it mean to you?

22. Tell me about any extra-curricular activities you participated in during high school (school newspaper, drama club, glee club).

23. Did you play sports in high school? If so, which sports? Was the sport (or sports) important to you? Why or why not?

24. If you played sports, tell me about the best game that you played. Why was it the best?

25. If you played sports, tell me about the worst game that you played. Why was it the worst?

26. Where did you attend college or another post-secondary school (if at all)?

27. Describe the campus.

28. What was your major in college (or another post-secondary school)? Why did you pick that major? When did you graduate?

29. Tell me about any special academic achievements while you were in college. Why were those achievements important to you?

30. What was it like going to that particular school? How many classes did you take each semester? What kinds of classes?

31. Tell me about any extra-curricular activities that you participated in during college or post-secondary school (sports; drama club; school newspaper).

32. Tell me about any unusual, interesting or amusing incidents that happened while you were in college or while you attended a post-secondary school.

33. What advice would you give to students who are in school today (either elementary students, high school students or college)?

Subject #3: Brothers/Sisters/Cousins

1. How many brothers and sisters do you have?

2. What are their names? Are they older or younger?

3. Tell me about your brothers and sisters. Any unusual, interesting or amusing incidents concerning your brothers and sisters?

4. Were (or are) you good friends with your brothers and sisters? Why or why not?

5. When and how did you spend the most time with your brothers and sisters when you were kids?

6. When you think about your brothers and sisters when you were children, how or where do you picture them? Why?

7. What is your <u>favorite</u> memory about your brothers and sisters?

8. What is your <u>least-favorite</u> memory concerning your brothers and sisters (an unpleasant experience, perhaps; was there a time when your brothers or sisters got you in trouble, for example)?

9. How often do you see your brothers and sisters? Are you close to them? Do you live close by? Do you have a close relationship? Why or why not?

10. How many cousins do you have?

11. What are their names? Are they older or younger?

12. Tell me about your cousins. Any unusual, interesting or amusing incidents concerning your cousins?

13. Were (or are) you good friends with your cousins? Why or why not?

14. When and how did you spend the most time with your cousins when you were kids?

15. When you think about your cousins when you were children, how or where do you picture them? Why?

16. What is your <u>favorite</u> memory about your cousins?

17. What is your <u>least-favorite</u> memory concerning your cousins (an unpleasant experience; was there a time when your cousins got you into trouble, for example)?

18. How often do you see your cousins? Are you close to them? Do you live close by? Do you have a close relationship? Why or why not?

Subject #4: Mother

1. What is/was your mother's first name? Maiden name?

2. Who was your mother named after, if anyone?

3. Where did your mother grow up?

4. Who were your mother's parents? Where did they grow up? Where were they from?

5. Tell me about your mother's parents. Did you know them very well? When did you see them?

6. Describe your mother. What color were/are her hair and eyes? Is she (or was she) tall or short? What was unique about her physical appearance?

7. Tell me about any unusual or amusing or interesting incidents that happened concerning your mother.

8. What stories did your mother tell about her own childhood (if any)?

9. Was your mother strict or easy-going when you were growing up, and what things did she do to show that she was strict or easy going?

10. What was your mother's occupation? Did she enjoy it? How long in that occupation?

11. What were your mother's feelings about cleaning and housekeeping? What things did she do to communicate her feelings? Any unusual or amusing incidents concerning housekeeping or cleaning?

12. What were your mother's feelings about food and cooking? What things did she do to communicate her feelings? Any unusual, interesting or amusing incidents concerning food or cooking?

13. What ways did your mother use to show you that she loved you?

14. How or where did your parents meet?

15. When and where were your folks married? Large or small wedding?

16. What were/are some of your mother's favorite sayings or pieces of wisdom that she passed along to you? When did she say them? Under what circumstances?

17. What clothes did your mother like to wear? Did she like to dress up? Wear jewelry? Perfume?

18. What piece of clothing that your mother wore do you remember best and why?

19. What piece of jewelry that your mother wore do you remember best and why?

20. Who were your mother's best friends? When did she see them? Any amusing, interesting or unusual incidents concerning your mother's best friends?

21. What were your mother's hobbies? How much time she spend on her hobbies? Any amusing, interesting or unusual incidents concerning your mother's hobbies?

22. What activities did you do with your mother? Did you help with the housework? Cooking? Dishes? Go shopping together?

23. How did you feel about doing those activities with your mother? Why did you feel that way?

24. What do you remember most about your mother? When you think about your mother, where do you picture her?

25. What is your best/favorite memory of your mother?

26. What is your worst memory associated with your mother? Was there a time when she was especially angry with you, for example?

27. If your mother has passed away, how did she die?

28. What do you remember about her funeral?

29. What did it mean to you to lose your mother? How old were you?

Subject #5: Father

1. What is/was your father's first name? Middle name? Last name?

2. Who was your father named after, if anyone?

3. Who were your father's parents? Where did they come from? Were they immigrants? From what country? When?

4. Tell me about your father's parents. What do you remember about them? Did you know them very well? When did you see them?

5. Where did your father grow up?

6. What stories did your father tell about his own childhood?

7. Describe your father's physical appearance.

8. What was unique about your father's physical appearance?

8. Describe your father's personality. What was unique about his personality?

9. Tell me about any unusual or amusing or interesting incidents concerning your father.

10. What was your father's occupation? How many years did he work at that occupation? Did he enjoy it? If so, why?

11. What was/are your father's feelings about food and cooking? Cleaning? Housekeeping? How did you know he felt that way? Any unusual or amusing or interesting incidents concerning your father and food/cooking, cleaning/housekeeping?

12. How did your father show that he loved you?

13. What are/were some of your father's favorite sayings?

14. What did you learn from your father's favorite sayings?

15. What clothes did your father like to wear? Why?

16. What is your favorite or best memory associated with an article of clothing that your father wore?

17. Who were your father's best friends? When did he spend time with them?

18. What were/are your father's hobbies? How much time did he spend on his hobbies? Did you share any of your father's hobbies with him?

19. What activities did you do with your father when you were a kid? Did you enjoy it? Why or why not?

20. What do you remember most about your father?

21. How do you picture your father when you think about him?

22. What is your best (favorite) memory of your father?

23. What your worst memory associated with your father? Was there a time when he was especially angry with you?

24. If your father has passed away, how did he die?

25. What do you remember about his funeral? What did it mean to you to lose your father?

Subject #6: Childhood Home

1.Tell me about the house where you lived when you were a kid. Where was it? How many rooms did it have? What color was it?

2. What could you see from the windows of the house where you grew up?

3. Tell me about the memories associated with the things you could see from the window of the house where you grew up.

4. What did you like <u>best</u> about the house where you grew up? Why?

5. What did you like <u>least</u> about the house where you grew up? Why?

6. What was the <u>best</u> thing that happened to you when you were living in the house where you grew up? Why was it the best?

7. What was the <u>worst</u> thing that happened to you when you were living in the house where you grew up? Why was it the worst?

8. Tell me about the bedroom you had when you were a kid. What color was it? How big was it? What furniture? How many windows? Did you share the bedroom with anyone?

9. What did you like about the bedroom you had when you were growing up?

10. What did you dislike about the bedroom you had when you were growing up?

11. Tell me about the history of the house where you grew up (if you know any of the history).

12. What happened to the house where you grew up? Is it still there or has it been torn down?

13. If the house has been torn down, how do you feel about that? Do you miss seeing it? Are you sorry it was torn down? Why or why not?

14. If the house has not been torn down, have you been back to see the place where you grew up? When? For what occasions? Do you stay at the house? Is it owned by a family member?

15. What memories are brought back when you see or visit the house where you grew up?

Subject #7: Wedding Day

1. Where or how did you meet your spouse?

2. How long have you been (or how long were) you married?

3. When is your wedding anniversary?

4. Why did you pick that particular date to get married? Is there a story associated with your wedding date?

5. Tell me about your wedding ceremony. Long or short? Elaborate or simple?

6. How many bridesmaids or groomsmen did you have? What were their names? What was their relationship to you? Friends? Relatives?

7. Why did you pick those people to be bridesmaids or groomsmen?

8. What did you wear on your wedding day? How much did it cost? Why did you select it? How did you find it?

9. How many guests were at your wedding? Who do you remember best from among all of the guests? Why?

10. Tell me about your wedding reception, if you had a wedding reception. Where was it held? What was on the menu? Why did you select that particular place for your reception?

11. Describe your wedding cake (if you had a wedding cake). How was it decorated? Did you save the top tier to eat on your first wedding anniversary? Why or why not?

12. Tell me about any unusual, interesting or amusing incidents that occurred on your wedding day.

13. Tell me about some of the wedding gifts you received.

14. What was your <u>favorite</u> wedding gift? Why?

15. What was your <u>least-favorite</u> wedding gift? Why?

16. What was the <u>best</u> thing that happened on your wedding day?

17. What was the <u>worst</u> thing that happened on your wedding day?

Subject # 8: Spouse/Marriage

1. Tell me about your husband/wife (physical appearance, personality, values, good qualities/bad qualities, likes/dislikes).

2. What do you (or did you) value the most about your spouse?

3. How/where did you meet?

4. Where did you go when you were dating?

5. How or when did you decide to get married?

6. Tell me about your early married life. Where did you live (city/state)? For how long?

7. Describe your "first house" (the first house you lived in as husband and wife).

8. Tell me about the activities you have enjoyed doing together. Why did you enjoy those activities?

9. Tell me about any unusual, amusing or interesting incidents concerning your spouse.

10. How was married life different later on from when you were first married?

11. What's your best memory of your spouse? When you think about your spouse, how do you picture him or her?

12. Tell me about your happiest times together. Why were/are they the happiest?

13. Tell me about the worst times you spent together (economic hardship; illness; other calamities). Why were/are they worst of times?

14. What hobbies do you (or did you) share with your spouse?

15. Tell me about a time when you are/were especially glad that your spouse is/was there (perhaps it was a time when your spouse was helpful in some way).

16. What have you learned from your spouse?

17. What has your spouse learned from you?

18. What have you been able to accomplish together, as a team, that you would not have been able to do alone?

19. What advice would you give to young people about choosing a spouse?

20. What advice would you give to young people about being a spouse?

Subject # 9: Adult Home

1. Tell me about the place or places where you have lived since you've been an adult. (city/state)

2 Tell me about the house (or houses) in which you have lived since you've been an adult.

3. Why did you live in that particular place or that particular house or houses (because of a job or for some other reason)?

4. Describe the house (or houses) that you have lived in. (Color, size, number of rooms).

5. What do (or did) you like best about a particular house where you have lived since you've been an adult?

6. What do (or did) you like least about the house (or houses) where you have lived since you've been an adult?

7. What is the best thing that happened to you in a particular house?

8. What is the worst thing that happened to you in a particular house?

Subject #10: Children

1. How many children do you have?

2. What are your children's names? When were they born?

3. Why or how did you choose those particular names for your children?

4. Where were your children born? Where were you living at the time?

5. What is memorable about your children's birthdays?

6. What are your <u>best</u> memories about your children? How do you picture your children when you think of them. What was the "best thing" your children did? Why was it the best?

7. What are your <u>worst</u> (most unpleasant or most negative) memories of your children? What was the "most terrible" thing your children did? Why was it the worst?

8. What were your children's favorite foods when they were growing up?

9. What were your children's favorite games when they were growing up?

10. What were your children's favorite clothes when they were growing up?

11. What were your children's favorite toys when they were growing up?

12. Who were your children's friends when they were kids? Did you approve? Why or why not?

13. What activities did you do with your children? Recreational activities? Work activities? Hobbies? Chores around the house?

14. What did you learn from your children?

15. What did you hope to teach your children? Why was that important to you?

16. What do you think your children learned from you?

17. Tell me about something that happened when your children were little.

18. Tell me about something that happened when your children were in high school.

19. Tell me about something that happened after your children were adults.

20. Tell me your favorite story about your children.

21. If you had it to do over again, would have children again? Why or why not?

22. How often to do you see your children now? Where do you see them? When? On what occasions?

23. What advice would you give to parents today?

Subject # 11: Birthdays

1. What do you associate most with birthdays? A party? A birthday cake? Gifts? Something else? Why?

2. Which birthday that you celebrated as a child do you remember the best? Why?

3. Describe the <u>best</u> birthday gift that you received as a child. Why was it the best?

4. Describe the <u>worst</u> birthday gift that you received as a child. Why was it the worst?

5. How many birthday parties did you have as a child? Many? Few? None? Why?

6. Tell me about the birthday parties that you had when you were a kid (if you had birthday parties).

7. Describe the <u>best</u> birthday gift that you have received as an <u>adult</u>. Why was it the best?

8. Describe the <u>worst</u> birthday gift that you received as an adult. Why was it the worst?

9. Tell me about the birthday parties that you have had since you've been an adult (if any).

10. What's your favorite kind of birthday cake? Why is it your favorite?

11. Tell me about the birthday cakes you had when you were a kid. Did someone bake a birthday cake for you every year? Why or why not?

12. Did you bake a birthday cake for someone when you were a child? If so, did someone help you? Who? How did the cake turn out?

13. If you have baked birthday cakes for others as an adult, for whom do you (or did you) make the cakes? Were the cakes elaborate or simple? Why?

14. If you've baked birthday cakes (either as a child or an adult), tell me about the <u>best</u> one you've ever made.

17. If you've baked birthday cakes (either as a child or an adult), tell me about the <u>worst</u> one you've ever made. What happened to it? Why was it the worst?

Subject #12: Spring

1. Describe the way you feel about the spring.

2. What was spring like when you were a child? Weather? Activities? Games? Where did you live?

3. What did spring mean to you when you were a child? Freedom from school? Baseball? Snow melting?

6. Tell me about something that happened during the spring when you were a child.

7. What other memories do you have about spring when you were a child?

4. What does spring mean to you as an adult? Weather? Activities? Gardening? Flowers? Snow melting?

8. Tell me about something that has happened during the spring after you became an adult.

9. What other memories do you have about spring?

10. What's the best thing that's happened during the spring, either when you were a child or an adult? Why was it the best?

11. What's the worst thing that's happened during the spring, either when you were a child or an adult? Why was it the worst?

Subject #13: Summer

1. Describe the way you feel about summer.

2. What was summer like when you were a child? Weather? Activities? Where did you live?

3. What did summer mean to you when you were a child? Freedom from school? Baseball? Other games? Gardens? Swimming?

4. Tell me about something that happened during the summer when you were a child.

6. What other memories do you have about summer when you were a child?

7. How has summer changed from the time you were a child and the way that summer is now? Is the weather different? Do you live in a different climate? Are your activities different?

8. Tell me about something that has happened to you during the summer since you've been an adult.

9. What's the <u>best</u> thing that's happened during the summer, either when you were a child or an adult? Why was it the best?

10. What's the <u>worst</u> thing that's happened during the summer, either when you were a child or an adult? Why was it the worst?

Subject #14: Fall/Autumn

1. Describe the way you feel about autumn. What do you like or dislike about autumn?

2. What was autumn like when you were a child? Weather? Activities? Where did you live?

3. What did autumn mean to you when you were a child? Going back to school? Colored leaves? Halloween?

4. Tell me about something that happened to you during the autumn when you were a child.

5. What other memories do you have about autumn when you were a child?

6. What does autumn mean to you as an adult? Weather? Activities?

7. Tell me about something that has happened during the autumn when you were an adult.

8. What other memories do you have about autumn?

9. What's the <u>best</u> thing that's happened to you during the autumn, either when you were a child or an adult? Why was it the best?

10. What's the <u>worst</u> thing that's happened to you during the autumn, either when you were a child or an adult? Why was it the worst?

Subject #15: Winter

1. Describe the way you feel about winter. What do you like or dislike about winter?

2. What was winter like when you were a child? Weather? Activities? Where did you live? Problems getting to school?

3. What did winter mean to you when you were a child? School? Games? Sledding? Skiing? Snow?

6. Tell me about something that happened during the winter when you were a child.

7. What other memories do you have about winter when you were a child?

8. What does winter mean to you as an adult? Weather? Activities?

9. How has winter changed from the time you were a child and the way that winter is now? Is the weather different? Do you live in a different climate? Are your activities different?

10. Tell me about something that has happened during the winter when you were an adult.

9. What's the best thing that's happened to you during the winter, either when you were a child or an adult? Why was it the best?

10. What's the worst thing that's happened to you during the winter, either when you were a child or an adult? Why was it the worst?

Subject #16: Easter

1. Did your family celebrate Easter when you were a child? Why or why not?

2. If your family observed Easter when you were a child, tell me about the way you celebrated the holiday.

3. What did you have to eat at Easter dinner when you were a child (if your family observed the holiday)?

4. Which food that was served at Easter did you like best? Why?

5. Which food that was served at Easter did you like least? Why?

6. What else did you do to celebrate Easter when you were a child, if anything?

8. If your family observed Easter when you were a child, who attended Easter dinner (if you had special Easter dinners)?

9. Tell me about any unusual, amusing or interesting incidents that occurred at Easter when you were a child.

10. Tell me what else you remember related to Easter, either when you were a child or after you became an adult.

Subject #17: Fourth of July

1. What did the Fourth of July mean to you when you were a kid?

2. Tell me about how the Fourth of July was celebrated when you were growing up.

3. Were there any unusual, amusing or interesting incidents that occurred on the Fourth of July when you were a child?

4. Did you go on picnics on the Fourth of July when you were a kid? Why or why not?

5. Tell me about any fireworks displays that you saw on the Fourth of July when you were a kid.

6. Tell me about any parades you saw on the Fourth of July when you were a kid.

7. What was the best Fourth of July, either when you were a kid or when you were an adult? Why was it the best?

8. What was the worst Fourth of July, either when you were a kid or when you were an adult? Why was it the worst?

9. Tell me what else you remember related to the Fourth of July, either when you were a child or when you were an adult.

Subject #18: Thanksgiving

1. What did Thanksgiving mean to you when you were a child?

2. How did you celebrate Thanksgiving when you were a child, if at all?

3. If your family celebrated Thanksgiving when you were a kid, what did you have to eat? Where was dinner served? At home? At a relative's house?

4. Which food that was served at Thanksgiving did you like the best? Why?

5. Which food that was served at Thanksgiving did you like the least? Why?

6. Tell me about any amusing, interesting or unusual incidents that have happened in connection with Thanksgiving (either when you were a child and after you became an adult).

7. Who made Thanksgiving dinner when you were a kid? Did you help make dinner? Why or why not?

8. How was your house decorated for Thanksgiving when you were a kid (if it was decorated at all)?

9. Describe the best Thanksgiving when you were a kid. Why was it the best?

10. Describe the worst Thanksgiving when you were a kid. Why was it the worst?

11. Describe the <u>best</u> Thanksgiving since you've been an adult. Why was it the best?

12. Describe the <u>worst</u> Thanksgiving since you've been an adult. Why was it the worst?

13. When you think about Thanksgiving, what immediately comes to mind? Something from your childhood? Something from later years? Sights? Smells? People?

14. How has Thanksgiving changed over the years? Differences in the kind of meal you make? Differences in the places where you celebrate Thanksgiving (for example, perhaps when you were a child you ate Thanksgiving dinner at your grandmother's house, but now you're the grandmother, and Thanksgiving is at your house)?

15. Tell me about something memorable that happened on the day after Thanksgiving or on the Saturday and Sunday following Thanksgiving. For example, if you've gone Christmas shopping the day after Thanksgiving, what was that like?

Subject #19: Christmas

1. What did Christmas mean to you when you were a kid?

2. How did you celebrate Christmas when you were a child (if at all)?

3. If your family celebrated Christmas when you were a kid, what did you have to eat?

4. Where was Christmas dinner served? At home? At a relative's house?

5. What did you do to celebrate Christmas Eve when you were a kid?

6. Which food that was served at Christmas did you like the best? Why?

7. Which food that was served at Christmas did you like the least? Why?

8. Who made Christmas dinner when you were a kid? Did you help? Why or why not?

9. How was your house decorated for Christmas when you were growing up?

10. Tell me about the Christmas trees that you had when you were a child.

11. Tell me about the Christmas programs you participated in when you were a kid. What was memorable about the programs?

12. Describe the best Christmas that you celebrated when you were a child. Why was it the best?

13. Describe the <u>worst</u> Christmas that you celebrated when you were a child. Why was it the worst?

14. Tell me about any interesting, unusual or amusing incidents that have happened in connection with Christmas (either when you were a kid or after you became an adult).

15. How has Christmas changed over the years? Differences in your activities? Differences in the kinds of gifts you give or receive?

16. Tell me about Christmases after you became an adult.

17. Describe the <u>best</u> Christmas you celebrated as an adult. Why was it the best?

18. Describe the <u>worst</u> Christmas you celebrated as an adult. Why was it the worst?

19. Tell me about any other memories you have concerning Christmas, either when you were growing up or after you became an adult.

Subject #20: Other Holidays

1. What other holidays were celebrated when you were a child (St. Patrick's Day, Valentine's Day, Halloween)?

2. Describe the other holidays that were celebrated when you were a child. How did you celebrate? What did you do? Where did you go?

3. Tell me about any holidays that you celebrated as a child that were related to the ethnic origin of your family or the ethnic origin of the area where you grew up. Which ethnic groups? Why were the celebrations important to your family or to the area where you lived?

4. Do you still celebrate any of those holidays today (St. Patrick's Day, Valentine's Day, Halloween, ethnic holidays, others)? Why or why not?

5. What did those holidays mean to you when you were a child?

6. What do those holidays mean to you as an adult?

Subject #21: War

1. Which wars do you remember? World War I? World War II? Korea? Vietnam? Others?

2. Why or how do you remember those wars? What do you remember about the war/wars?

3. What was the impact of war on your life? How did the war change you?

4. Were you a member of the Armed Forces? If so, did you volunteer or were you drafted? How old were you?

5. How long did you serve? Where did you serve? In what capacity?

6. Tell me about your experiences during the war (either in the Armed Services or as civilian).

7. Did you lose any family members in the war? Others? Community members? Friends?

8. If you served in the Armed Forces, would you do it again? Why or why not?

9. Do you believe it is important for people to serve their country in some capacity? Why or why not?

Subject #22: Pets

1. Do you like animals? Why or why not?

2. Tell me about the pets you had when you were a child.

3. Which pet that you had a child was your <u>favorite</u>. Why was it your favorite? What did you like about it?

4. Which pet that you had as a child was your <u>least</u> <u>favorite</u>? What didn't you like about it?

5. Tell me about the pets you've had since you've become an adult.

6. Which pet that you've had since you've been an <u>adult</u> has been your <u>favorite</u> (if any)? Why?

7. What do animals mean to your life, if anything?

8. How are animals or pets related to your hobbies? To your occupation (if at all)?

9. Tell me about any other amusing, unusual or interesting things that have happened in connection with your pets, either when you were growing up or after you became an adult.

Subject #23: Hobbies

1. What are your favorite hobbies? Why?

2. When did you start your hobby?

4. Why did you choose your hobby?

5. What hobbies did you have as a child?

6. What hobbies did you share your with your brothers/sisters or mother/father or cousins (if any)? Why?

9. What are some of your best/favorite memories associated with your hobby?

10. What are some of your worst memories associated with your hobby (such as an unpleasant experience)?

12. What's the best thing that's happened to you because of your hobby?

13. What's the worst thing that's happened to you because of your hobby or in association with your hobby?

14. Tell me about any other unusual, amusing or interesting incidents concerning your hobby or hobbies.

Subject #24: Food

1. What's your favorite food (or foods)? Why? What's special about your favorite food?

2. What was your favorite food (or foods) when you were a kid? Why? What was special about it?

3. When did you eat your favorite food (or foods) when you were a kid?

4. When do you eat your favorite food now?

5. Who made your favorite food when you were growing up?

6. Who else in your family, when you were a kid, liked your favorite food?

7. What did your brothers and sisters think of your favorite food? If they liked it, too, did you fight over it? What happened when you got into fights?

8. What's your best/favorite memory associated with your favorite food? Why?

10. What's the worst/most unpleasant memory associated with food or your favorite food (if any)? Why?

11. Tell me about any unusual, interesting or amusing incidents concerning your favorite food (or food in general).

Subject #25: Occupation/Work

1. What occupations have you had?

2. How long did you work at your job (or jobs)?

3. Why did you choose that particular job or jobs?

4. Describe the education you needed for the occupation or jobs.

6.What jobs did you have when you were growing up (if any)? How much were you paid? What did you buy with the money you earned?

7. What were salary ranges, in general, when you were a child (either for kids or adults)? How much did people earn a day? A week? A month? A year?

8. Tell me about any interesting, unusual or amusing incidents that happened in connection with a job that you had when you were or growing or with a job that you had as an adult.

9. What was the <u>best</u> thing that happened to you while working a particular job (either as a child or as an adult)?

10. What was the <u>worst</u> thing that happened to you while working a particular job (either as a child or as an adult)?

11. What was your <u>favorite</u> job? Why?

12. What was your <u>least-favorite</u> job? Why?

15. If you had it to do all over again, would you work the same job (or jobs)? Why or why not?

Subject #26: Illness and Injuries

1. What illnesses and injuries have you suffered in your life?

2. Describe the <u>worst</u> illness or injury you've had. Why was it the worst?

3. Describe the <u>worst</u> illness you had as a child. Why was it the worst? How long were you sick? How did you get well?

4. Describe the <u>worst</u> injury you had as a child. What happened? How long did it take you to recover?

5. When you were a kid, who took care of you when you were sick or injured? What did that person do to help you feel better?

6. Did you see a doctor when you were a kid if you were sick or injured? Why or why not?

7. What medicines did you take when you were a kid? How did you feel about taking medicine? Did it help?

8. What kinds of salves or ointments did you use on cuts and scrapes when you were a kid? Was it something that was purchased? A homemade remedy? Did it help?

9. What illnesses or injuries did your brothers and sisters have when you were a kid?

10. What illnesses or injuries did your mother or father suffer when you were a kid?

11. What illnesses or injuries did your grandparents suffer when you were a kid?

19. What homemade remedies did your mother and father use for themselves when you were a kid? For which illnesses or injuries? Did you use those remedies too? Did they help?

20. What homemade remedies did your grandparents use, if any? For which illnesses or injuries? Did the remedies help?

21. What "commercial" salves, ointments or medications do you remember from when you were a kid (mercurochrome, for example)? What was good or bad about the salves, ointments or medications? Did they help?

22. What do you remember about doctors making house calls (if in fact, you do remember doctors making house calls)? Do you believe house calls were a good idea? Why or why not?

23. Tell me about the doctor in your hometown (if your hometown had a doctor).

24. How have medical treatments changed over the years? Are the changes you have observed or experienced good or bad? Why?

Subject #27: Friends

1. Who was your best friend when you were a kid? Describe that person. What did he or she look like?

2. Why was that person your best friend?

3. Tell me about any unusual, interesting or amusing incidents concerning your best friend.

4. What was the most fun you had with your best friend when you were a kid?

5. What activities did you do with your best friend?

6. When did you get to see your best friend?

7. How did you meet your best friend?

8. What is your best/favorite memory of the person who was your best friend when you were a kid?

9. What is your worst (most negative or unpleasant) memory of the person who was your best friend when you were a kid? Did you get into any trouble together, for example? What happened?

10. Are you still friends with your best friend from childhood? If so, when do you see each other? Do you talk on the telephone? Write letters?

11. Tell me about any other best friends that you've had over the years.

Subject #28: Neighbors

1. Tell me about the neighbors you had when you were a kid.

2. Tell me about the neighborhood where you grew up.

3. Describe the houses that your neighbors lived in. What was memorable about the houses? What was memorable about the yards around your neighbors' houses?

4. When did you visit your neighbors? Did you visit them often? Why or why not?

5. What is your best/favorite memory of the neighbors you had when you were a kid?

6. What is your worst (most unpleasant) memory of the neighbors you had as a kid?

7. Which neighbor do you remember the best from your childhood? Why?

8. Tell me about the neighbors that you've had since you've been an adult.

9. What is your best memory of the neighbors you've had since you've been an adult? Why is it your best memory?

10. What is your worst (most unpleasant) memory of the neighbors you've had since you've been an adult? What happened? Why is it the worst?

Subject #29: Church/Religion

1. What role did church/religion play in your life when you were a child?

2. Why was church important to your family when you were a child, if it was important?

3. What memories do you have from your childhood about church/religion? Sunday school? Christmas programs? Other events?

4. If you attended church as a child, what did the church look like? Where was it? How did you get there? Did you walk? Or did you go by motorized transportation?

5. If you attended church as a child, which people do you remember from church? What is memorable about them? Why?

6. What role has church/religion played in your life since you've been an adult?

7. What memories do you have about church/religion since you've been an adult?

8. Tell me about the people who have belonged to your church since you've been an adult. What is memorable about them? Why?

Subject #30: Changes

1. What changes have you observed or experienced in your lifetime (such as changes in society, culture, marriage, wages, electricity, schools, telephones, roads, cars, the cost of housing, advances in technology)?

2. What historical events have you observed or experienced in your lifetime (for example, the Great Depression, World War II, other wars, Americans landing on the moon, the assassinations of President John F. Kennedy, Robert Kennedy, Martin Luther King)?

3. Tell me about the historical events you have observed or experienced. Where were you when they occurred? How did you learn about the events (television, newspaper, radio, word-of-mouth)? What impact did the historical events have on you?

4. What is the most important change you have experienced? Why is it the most important? How has it changed your life?

5. What was the best thing about "the good old days?"

6. What was the worst thing about "the good old days?"

About the Author

LeAnn R. Ralph earned a Bachelor of Arts in English with a writing emphasis from the University of Wisconsin-Whitewater and also earned a Master of Arts in Teaching from UW-Whitewater.

She is the former editor of the *Wisconsin Regional Writer* (the quarterly publication of the Wisconsin Regional Writers' Assoc.) and is the author of the books, *Christmas In Dairyland (True Stories From a Wisconsin Farm)* (Aug. 2003), *Give Me a Home Where the Dairy Cows Roam* (Sept. 2004), *Cream of the Crop* (Oct. 2005), and *Where the Green Grass Grows* (Oct. 2006).

LeAnn lives in Wisconsin on part of the farm where she grew up with her husband and assorted dogs, cats and horses.

To read sample chapters of her books, other Rural Route 2 stories, to see what readers are saying about *Christmas in Dairyland* and *Give Me a Home Where the Dairy Cows Roam,* and *Cream of the Crop* and *Where the Green Grass Grows*—or to sign up for LeAnn's e-mail newslettet—Rural Route 2 News, visit—www.ruralroute2.com

****

Questions? Comments? If so, you can e-mail LeAnn at mailto:bigpines@ruralroute2.com

****

Need Help Editing Your Manuscript?

After you have interviewed your list of people and have transcribed your interviews, if you would like someone to edit the manuscript, I am available for hire.

Manuscripts can be e-mailed to me in the body of the e-mail, as an Apple Works attachment or as a Microsoft attachment.

The rate for editing manuscripts is 1 cent per word. Word count is calculated on the total number of words you submit (unedited). For example, if your manuscript is 50 pages with 350 typed words per page, the cost for editing would be $175.

If you submit a 100-page manuscript with 350 typed words per page, the cost for editing would be $350.

If your manuscript is 150 pages with 350 typed words per page, the cost for editing would be $525.

Turn-around time on editing depends upon the length of the manuscript. In most cases, the manuscript will be finished within a month of receiving it.

Once the full manuscript is edited, I will send you an invoice, and after payment is received, I will e-mail the manuscript back to you.

I will also be happy to do a 'sample edit' of 5 pages of your manuscript, for free, to help you decide whether you want the manuscript edited.

If you have questions, feel free to e-mail me at —
bigpines@ruralroute2.com

Or you can call me at (715) 962-3368

Best wishes on gathering your family stories and writing your ora
histories!

****

Printed in the United States
130890LV00002B/388/A

9 781601 452399